Great Outdoors GAMES & PUZZLES

Bring the **Outdoors Inside** with 100 Mazes, Word Games, Picture Puzzles, Jokes & Riddles, Brainteasers, and Fun-Packed Activities

Helene Hovanec & Patrick Merrell

Illustration and design by
Patrick Merrell

The mission of Storey Publishing is to serve our customers by publishing practical information that encourages personal independence in harmony with the environment.

Edited by Lisa H. Hiley
Illustration and design by Patrick Merrell
Art direction and cover design by Vicky Vaughn Design
Production assistance by Kristy L. MacWilliams

Storey books are available for special premium and promotional uses and for customized editions. For further information, please call 1-800-793-9396.

Printed in the United States by Versa Press
10 9 8 7 6 5 4 3 2 1

CONTENTS

Wow! All this cool stuff is inside.

Plus US!

SPECIAL 3 SECTION

A DAY AT THE COUNTY FAIR

Instructions

This book is divided into five sections that will take you on a trip through the great outdoors. The puzzles become more challenging as you go, so you might want to start at the beginning and work your way through. Or you can pick and choose the ones that look like the most fun.

You're in for a treat starting on page 51. You'll find a special section there — A Day at the County Fair!

On page 113, you'll find a Great Outdoors Dictionary. It's set up like a quiz and has many of the words that are used in this book. You can try it before you do the puzzles — or after, when you've already seen the words in action. It's up to you!

Here are a couple of suggestions:

- Use a pencil in case you need to erase anything.
- There a few games made for two people, so have a friend, parent, or brother or sister join in the fun on those ones. You can do all the puzzles by yourself, but sometimes it's fun to do them with another person.
- The answers start on page 119, and it's okay to peek if you need a hint.

Have a great time in the great outdoors! Let's get going . . .

Hey, wait for me!

A COUNTRY STROLL

Easy Puzzles to Get You Going

DIFFICULTY RATING:
1 LOG

The puzzles in this section are almost as easy as falling off a log!

I'd rather sit on a log when I solve puzzles.

ROCKY ROAD

Which path will lead Buckley and Daffodil to Big Rock?

TAKE A HIKE

Get ready to take a hike by gathering the items below and putting them into the grid. Use the letters that are already filled in to help you place each word or phrase. One word will lead to another until the whole grid is filled in.

BACKPACK   FLASHLIGHT   MAP
COMPASS   FOOD   WATER
HIKING BOOTS

CHECK THIS OUT

Circle all the words with a ✔ in front of them. Then read the circled words from the top down to find a riddle and answer.

✖ WHEN ✔ WHAT ● WHY ★ WHO ▼ WHERE ■ WHOM

▼ MOVER ★ MOOSE ✖ MONKEY ● MOLE ■ MOTOR ✔ MOVIE

★ DID ✔ DOES ● DIDN'T ✖ DON'T ▼ COULD ■ DO

■ THE ✖ THOSE ● AN ▼ THAT ★ THEIR ✔ A

▼ RAPTOR ● CHICKEN ★ FROG ✖ TOAD ✔ REPTILE ■ GOAT

✔ LIKE ✖ DISLIKE ▼ LOVE ■ HATE ● FEEL ★ SENSE

▼ MOST? ★ WORST? ■ LEAST? ✔ BEST? ✖ LESS? ● MORE?

● A ★ AN ✔ THE ▼ THAT ✖ THOSE ■ THESE

■ FISH ▼ BEE ★ MOTH ✔ LIZARD ✖ DUCK ● CRICKET

✖ WITH ✔ OF ▼ UNDER ● ABOVE ■ OFF ★ BETWEEN

■ OX ★ OW ● OR ▼ ON ✔ OZ ✖ OKAY

POND VISITOR

There's someone already in the pond. Connect the dots to decide if it's an animal that belongs in a country pond.

Start

ORDER! ORDER!

Can you put these four pictures in order so that they make sense?
Write numbers from 1 to 4 in the circles.

THREESIES

10

Cross off every letter that appears in the grid THREE times.
Then put the leftover letters in the blank spaces below. Go from
left to right and top to bottom to find the answer to this riddle:

What insect tastes good on toast?

H	A	M	V	X	V	G
M	H	M	X	V	X	B
S	H	S	U	T	Q	G
S	K	T	P	P	Q	G
K	K	Q	I	P	E	C
J	R	J	I	F	D	C
D	J	L	I	D	Y	C

Riddle answer:

__ __ __ __ __ __ " __ __ __ __ __ " __ __ __

LOOK AROUND

Circle seven things on the next page that are different from the scene on this page.

11

HEADING HOME

A game for 2, 3, or 4 players using one die. Make marks (your initials, for example) to keep track of what space you're on.

1. Pick an animal and make your mark on the START square.
2. Youngest player goes first and rolls the die.
3. Each animal has a number. If your roll is the same as your animal's number, move ahead one square. You can also move ahead one square if you roll a 5 or 6—those are wild!
4. If your roll is not your number, or a 5 or 6, you can't move. Roll only once per turn.
5. Now the next player takes a turn.
6. The first one to arrive HOME wins!

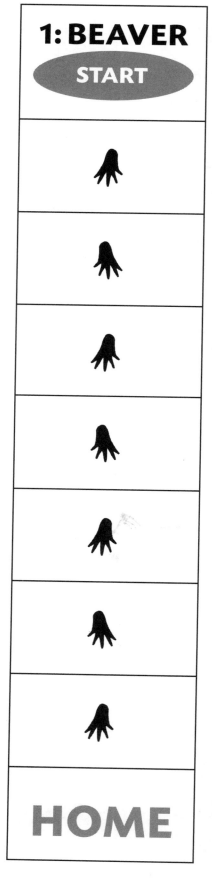

1: BEAVER

START

HOME

2: BEAR	3: FOX	4: DUCK
START	START	START

HOME   HOME   HOME

12

WHAT IS IT?

Buckley and Daffodil heard something loud on their walk.
Color in every shape with a ★ in it to see what made the noise.
Color in every shape with a ● in it to spell its name.

EYE CATCHERS

13

One letter of the alphabet is missing in each grid. Write the missing letter in the numbered spaces below. Then read across to find a red-eyed bird that makes a tiny nest.

1

E	S	R	Q	P
F	D	T	U	O
G	W	C	X	N
H	Y	Z	B	M
I	J	K	L	A

4

L	K	A	U	V
M	J	B	T	W
N	I	C	S	X
O	H	D	R	Y
P	G	F	Q	Z

2

V	W	X	Y	Z
U	T	S	R	Q
A	B	C	D	E
K	J	H	G	F
L	M	N	O	P

5

E	F	G	H	I
M	D	L	K	J
N	P	C	Q	R
V	U	T	B	S
W	X	Y	Z	A

3

V	U	K	J	A
W	T	L	I	B
X	S	M	H	C
Y	Q	N	G	D
Z	P	O	F	E

V I R E O
1 2 3 4 5

FINE DINING

Follow the cross-out directions for the letters in the grid. Then write the LEFTOVER letters on the lines below. Go from left to right and top to bottom to find the answer to this riddle:

What do frogs eat for lunch?

Cross out:

4 A's

2 B's

4 G's

4 J's

3 M's

3 O's

4 P's

5 T's

4 V's

3 W's

2 X's

3 Y's

4 Z's

P	Z	Z	Y	F	B	B
R	Z	Z	Y	Y	T	E
P	V	N	G	T	W	W
P	V	V	T	C	W	H
P	F	T	X	X	M	M
O	T	V	L	G	I	M
O	O	E	G	J	J	A
A	A	G	J	J	S	A

Answer:

__ __ __ __ __ __ __ __ __

BIRDS IN THE SKY

While Buckley was out bird-watching, he made silhouettes (black outline drawings) of all the birds he saw. After he was done, he noticed he'd drawn two of every type of bird except for one. Can you find and circle the one silhouette in his sketchbook that doesn't have an exact match?

MOVE IT

Move the letters listed below to the correct spaces. For example, A gets moved to space 7. When all the letters have been moved, you will have the answer to this riddle:

What is a bird's favorite dessert?

LETTERS

A = 7

C = 1, 4, 10, 15

E = 9, 20

H = 2, 11

I = 12, 19

K = 18

L = 6

O = 3, 5, 16, 17

P = 14

R = 13

S = 21

T = 8

Just fill in these letters below.

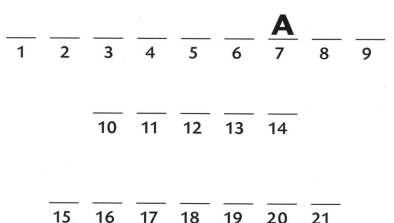

The answer

to the riddle:

___ ___ ___ ___ ___ ___ **A** ___ ___
 1   2   3   4   5   6   7   8   9

___ ___ ___ ___ ___
10 11 12 13 14

___ ___ ___ ___ ___ ___ ___
15 16 17 18 19 20 21

I already filled in the A.

2

ACROSS THE CREEK

Rivers of Fun Stuff

DIFFICULTY RATING:

2 LOGS

17 RAFTING FUN

Buckley and Daffodil are taking a little trip down the creek.
Can you help them find the way to Buckley's lodge?

BIRD-WATCHING

Each of the 10 birds listed below fits into one spot across the grid. Count the number of letters in each bird's name and then place it in the grid that has the same number of squares.

When all of the birds are entered, read DOWN the starred column to find something you need when you go bird-watching.

PURPLE MARTIN goes in the 12-square space.

And ROAD RUNNER goes in the 10-square space.

BLUEBIRD   ALBATROSS
SWALLOW   PURPLE MARTIN
CANARY   ROAD RUNNER
STORK   DOVE
JAY   MOCKINGBIRD

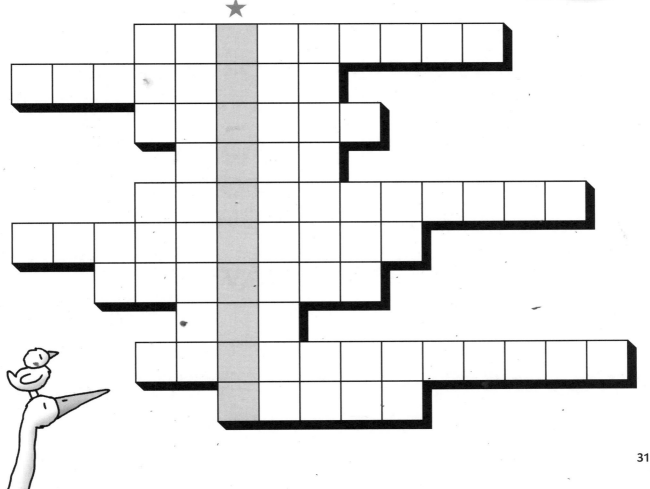

MIRROR MIRROR

Take a solving break! Hold this page up to a mirror to find three jokes and their answers.

Now that's a funny picture!

Uh…Buckley, it's you.

WHY WAS THE TURKEY ALLOWED TO JOIN THE BAND?

BECAUSE HE HAD THE DRUMSTICKS.

WHERE DO TURTLES EAT?

IN SLOW FOOD RESTAURANTS.

WHAT WOULD YOU GET IF YOU CROSSED A CENTIPEDE AND A PARROT?

A WALKIE-TALKIE.

Yak!

Yak!

Yak!

ROAD HOG

Put one letter into the blank space on each line to name a vehicle.
Then read down the starred column to answer this riddle:

What kind of vehicle does a hog drive in the country?

★

T _a_ X I C A B

_p_ O L I C E   C A R

F _i_ R E   E N G I N E

D U N E   B U _d_ G Y

B _u_ S

J E E _p_

T _T_ R A C T O R

T _R_ I C Y C L E

A M B _A_ L A N C E

_C_ A R

D I R T   B I _k_ E

33

UNDERWATER

Circle eight things on the next page that are different from the scene on this page.

JUST BEE-CAUSE

Change each letter below to the one that
comes just BEFORE it in the alphabet.

Write each new letter on the line above the original letter.
When you're done, you'll find two riddles and answers.

Here is a copy of the alphabet to guide you:

A B C D E F G H I J K L M N O P Q R S T U V W X Y Z

1
‾X‾I‾B‾U ‾J‾T ‾B ‾C‾F‾F‾'‾T

‾G‾B‾W‾P‾S‾J‾U‾F ‾D‾P‾V‾O‾U‾S‾Z?

‾T‾U‾J‾O‾H‾B‾Q‾P‾S‾F

2
‾X‾I‾B‾U ‾E‾P ‾Z‾P‾V

‾D‾B‾M‾M ‾B ‾C‾F‾F ‾U‾I‾B‾U

‾E‾P‾F‾T ‾O‾P‾U ‾C‾S‾B‾H?

‾B ‾I‾V‾N‾C‾M‾F ‾C‾F‾F

36

MESSAGE CENTER

Put the 10 words into the grid in alphabetical order from
A to J. Then write the circled letters into the blank spaces
below. Go from top to bottom to find the answer to this riddle:

How do you send a message in the forest?

DOZEN

HORSE

ERASE

JUICE

GECKO

ABOUT

FIRST

CLIMB

IDEAL

BUYER

Riddle answer: ___ ___   ___ ___ ___ ___ ___   ___ ___

37

"R" YOU READY?

RIVER and RAYS (from the sun) start with R. Can you find eight more things in this picture that begin with the letter R?

TREE TOPS

The trees in the box are hidden in the sentences below. To find them, look at the letters at the end of one word and join them to the beginning of the next word. (Some trees are even hidden among three words.) Underline each tree you find and cross it off the list like we did for CEDAR.

ASPEN	~~CEDAR~~	CYPRESS
LIME	FIR	OAK	PALM
PINE	PECAN	TEAK

THEY RA<u>CED AR</u>OUND THE TRACK.

IS THE HERO A KIND PERSON?

CAN YOU SPIN EIGHT TOPS?

HIS PEN PAL MIGHT VISIT.

LUCY PRESSED A HANDKERCHIEF.

WHO HAS PENCILS FOR THE TEACHER?

WHICH RECIPE CAN YOU MAKE?

WHERE IS THE TEA KETTLE?

I'LL BE THERE IF I REMEMBER.

WHERE WILL I MEET YOU?

25 CREATE A COMIC

Copy each drawing below, putting it in the correct box on the next page so that the cartoon makes sense. We've included a few drawing tips to help you.

1. Use a pencil to plan out how the characters will fit into each box.
2. Sketch in the basic, larger shapes first and then add the details like eyes and a mouth. (For example, see drawing A below.)
3. Go over your lines in pen, and then erase your pencil lines (make sure the pen lines have dried).
4. Color your comic in if you'd like.

26

POND GRASS

Start at the bottom and follow each piece of pond grass to find out which duck is nibbling on it. Write the numbers in the blanks after each letter.

A 4   B 3   C 1   D 2

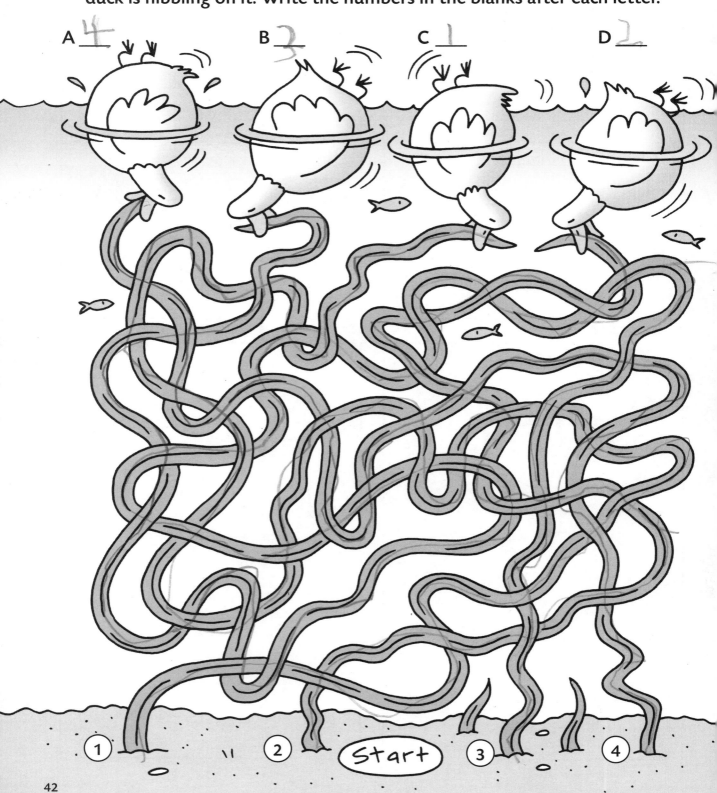

WATER FUN

Spending time in the great outdoors often includes water fun.
Here are 12 bodies of water where you can wade or swim.
Can you find and circle them in the grid? Look across, down,
and diagonally (on a slant), both forward and backward. BAY
is circled and crossed off the word list to get you started.

~~BAY~~
BROOK
CREEK
INLET
LAKE
OCEAN
POND
POOL
RIVER
SEA
SOUND
STREAM

```
B A Y  L O O P
N R E  K A L O
A Q O  E Z I N
E V S  O U N D
C R E  E K L X
O Z R  I V E R
Y M A  E R T S
```

43

FIND THE TWINS

Only two of the four DIVING otters (with numbers) are exactly the same and only two of the four SLIDING otters (with letters) are exactly the same. Can you spot the two sets of twins?

STOCKPILERS

On each line there is a 5-letter word in COLUMN A and a 4-letter word in COLUMN B. The letters in both words are the same except for one extra letter. Put that extra letter on the blank space on the middle line. Then read down to find a rodent that stuffs food in its cheeks. The first one has been done for you to get you started.

COLUMN A	EXTRA LETTER	COLUMN B
CEDAR	C	READ
BIRCH	___	CRIB
ROBIN	___	BORN
PETAL	___	LATE
MOLES	___	LOSE
MOUSE	___	SOME
NEWTS	___	WETS
PARKS	___	RAPS

Here's another animal that stockpiles food for the winter.

COLUMN A	EXTRA LETTER	COLUMN B
MAPLE	___	MEAL
PINES	___	PENS
TRACK	___	CART
CANOE	___	ONCE

45

DRAWING THE LINE

This is one of Buckley and Daffodil's favorite two-player games. They play by drawing grids on the ground, but you can use the grids we've included.

How to play:

1. Player one draws a line that goes up and down and connects two boxes.
2. Player two draws a line that goes side to side and connects two boxes.
3. Continue taking turns, always drawing your line in the same direction.
4. Once a box has a line drawn in it, another line can't be drawn in it.
5. The first player who can't draw a line loses.

Here's a sample game:

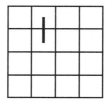 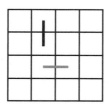 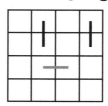 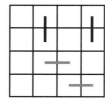 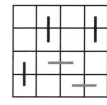

| Player 1 draws an up-and-down line in two boxes. | Player 2 draws a side-to-side line in two boxes. | Player 1 adds a second up-and-down line. | Player 2 adds a second side-to-side line. | Player 1 draws a line and wins! Player 2 can't put in a line. |

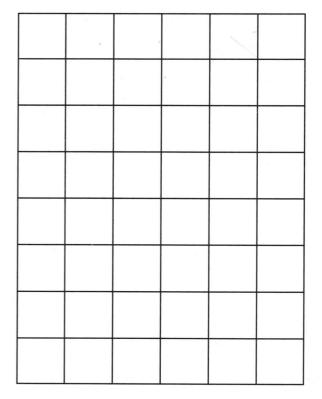

30 TREE-HEE-HEE

Buckley and Daffodil have mixed up all these jokes and their answers. Can you match them up? Write the number of the correct joke answer in the space after each letter.

A ___
What part of a yew tree (an evergreen) might be a reply to this statement: "I'd do it!"

B ___
Why was the big bank chain like a tree after a hurricane?

C ___
What do you get when you cross a quilled animal with an evergreen tree?

D ___
How can you identify a dogwood tree?

1. PORCUPINE CONES

2. FROM ITS LOUD BARK

3. IT HAD BRANCHES ALL OVER TOWN

4. YEW WOOD KNOT (You would not)

Tree Jokes
THIS END UP

48

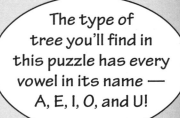

TREE-MENDOUS FACT

31

Follow the directions to find seven letters in the grid. After you find a letter, write it in the blank space. Then read down to find the largest tree in the world. It's called the "General Sherman" tree and is as high as a 27-story building.

FIND THE LETTER

That is above F and below L _____

That is between G and B _____

That is next to M and above Z _____

That is below V and above R _____

That is between Y and X _____

That is above D and next to R _____

That is below Z and above H _____

Q	M	W	C
Z	Y	O	X
A	V	T	L
H	U	J	S
I	R	P	F
D	G	E	B

DISCOVERY PATH

The 16 words on this list are all things you might see while walking through the woods. Can you find and circle them in the grid? Look across, down, and diagonally (on a slant), both forward and backward. ANT is circled and crossed off the word list to get you started.

ANT
BEAVER
BIRD
ELK
FERN
FOX
FROG
HARE
MOOSE
MOTH
NEST
NEWT
SNAKE
SQUIRREL
TRAIL
TREE

S M B I R D M
Q N E S T Y O
U E A X O F T
I W V K Z R H
R T E L E O A
R N R E F G R
E S O O M Z E
L I A R T N A

Bet you can't find me in the grid!

You're easy to find from where I'm sitting!

50

A DAY AT THE COUNTY FAIR

DIFFICULTY RATING:
3 LOGS

YAY! County fair puzzles!

Which is much better than county UNFAIR puzzles!

Hee hee.

BUZZ OFF

You may not be able to get rid of those bugs that bug you at county fairs, but you can laugh at them. Here's how: Unscramble the letter groups below to make real words. Write them on the lines. Then read the unscrambled words to find three insect riddles and their answers.

HTAW   IDD   TEH   EBE   ASY   OT   HET   LEROWF?

_____

HYE,   UBD,   HAWT   MIET   OD   OUY   ONEP?

_____

AWHT   AWS   EHT   PIREDS   ONGDI   TA   ETH   ARIF?

_____

INGKAM   A   BEW   ISTE.

_____

HATW   GUB   UMPSJ   VROE   ODSA   BLESTOT?

_____

A   LASGS   PERPOH.

_____

THAT RINGS A BELL

Each answer in this test of brain power is a pair of words that rhyme. For example, a chubby mammal that flies would be a FAT BAT. See if you can fill in all the words from BOTTOM to TOP and ring the bell.

(6) A flower that takes a nap is a
LAZY _____

(5) A young cat who tells jokes is a
WITTY _____

(4) A rabbit who tells jokes is a
FUNNY _____

(3) A platter of worms is a
FISH _____

(2) A fake horse is a
PHONY _____

(1) A shady place to swim is a
COOL _____

LIVESTOCK SHOW

A livestock show is a popular event where animals such as cattle, goats, sheep, horses, and pigs are shown and judged. All the words in the lists below are spelled with the letters in LIVESTOCK SHOW. Put each word into the grid. Start with the letters that are already in place and you will fill up the grid quickly.

3 Letters

LET
OIL
SIT

4 Letters

ECHO
HIKE
HISS
KITE
SHOE
WISH

5 Letters

STEWS
WITCH

6 Letters

CLOSET
TOWELS
VIOLET

7 Letters

LOCKETS
WHISTLE

WOO HOO! I LIKE THIS!

All those words you just said — each one uses letters from LIVESTOCK SHOW.

LIVESTOCK SHOW

DOG SHOW

Here's a riddle for you:

What kind of dog never ever barks?

To find the answer, write one letter in each blank to complete the name of a dog breed. Then read UP the starred column.

Best in Show

BEA __ LE

C __ LLIE

__ ACHSHUND

SAIN __ BERNARD

PO __ DLE

S __ EEPDOG

DALM __ TIAN

★

Longest in Show

PICTURE SUDOKU

Fill in the boxes using the different pictures. Each picture must appear only ONCE in each row going across, only ONCE in each column going up and down, and only ONCE in each group of four boxes (with the heavier outlines). Can you fill in the rest of the pictures?

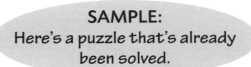

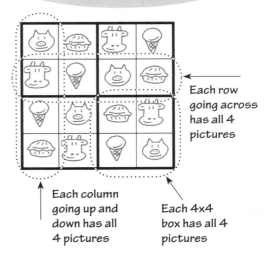

SAMPLE:
Here's a puzzle that's already been solved.

Each row going across has all 4 pictures

Each column going up and down has all 4 pictures

Each 4x4 box has all 4 pictures

In the grid above, the upper left square has to be a pig.

That's because the 3 squares below it are filled with the other 3 animals.

38 MISSING PIECES

This picture of Buckley and Daffodil at the "Old and New Tractor Exhibit" was accidentally cut up. Most of it has been put back together, but there are still five pieces missing. Write the letter of the correct pieces in the spaces.

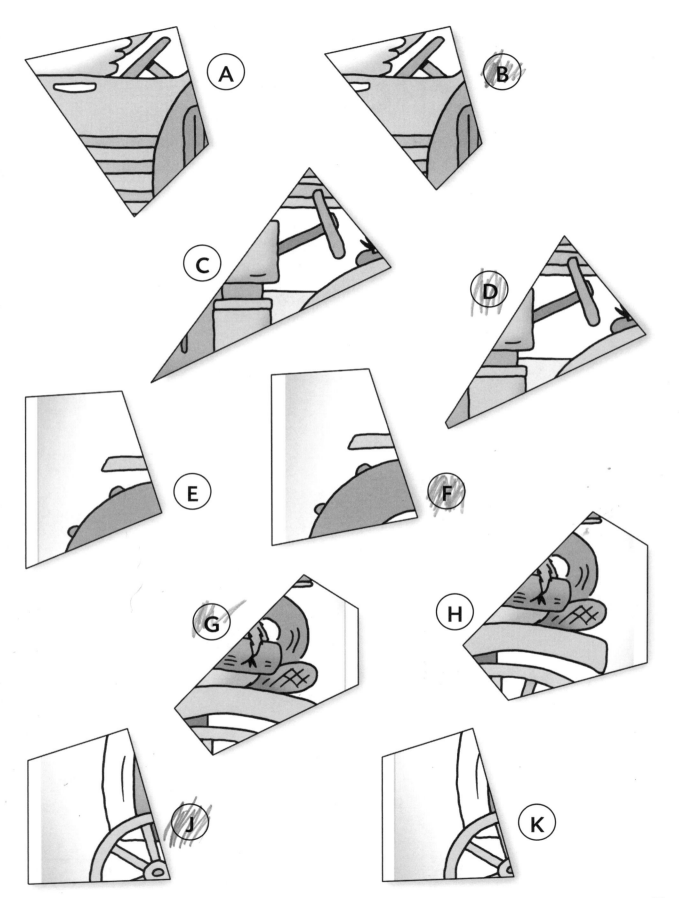

FOOD FOR THOUGHT

Fill in each blank space to make an ordinary seven-letter word. Then move the numbered letter from each word to the same-numbered blank at the bottom of the page. Read across to find a popular food found at county fairs.

PIC __ LES
9

FIR __ MAN
5

FOR __ VER
10

TRA __ FIC
1

SPI __ ACH
3

KET __ HUP
7

BLA __ KET
4

VIT __ MIN
8

ATH __ ETE
6

REQ __ EST
2

Popular food:

___ ___ ___ ___ ___ ___   ___ ___ ___ ___
1   2   3   4   5   6   7   8   9   10

HANDIWORK

Write the answer to each clue in the grid going either ACROSS or DOWN. Then fill in the numbered spaces at the bottom of the page with the letters found in the matching numbered squares. Read across to find some of the best-selling items at county fairs.

ACROSS

1. Take a break
3. Freezing
4. Item worn by a cook to protect clothes
5. Utensil used with a knife
6. Opposite of go ✓

DOWN

2. A train runs on this
3. Walking sticks

Answer: ___ ___ ___ ___ ___ ___
         3   1   4   5   2   6

61

TIN CAN TOSS

Hit the cans using a pencil!
1. Put your pencil point on softball A. 2. Close your eyes and draw a line to the stack of tin cans labeled A. 3. Stop drawing, open your eyes, and see how you did. Write your score in the first box below softball A. "Toss" three softballs at each target and total up your score.

INNER SPACE

On each line there is a six-letter word in COLUMN A and a five-letter word in COLUMN B. The letters in both words are the same except for one extra letter. Put that extra letter on the blank space in the middle line. Then read down to find the answer to this riddle:

Where does an astronaut keep his food when he goes to a county fair?

COLUMN A	EXTRA LETTER	COLUMN B
INSECT	_____	SCENT
ANSWER	_____	SWEAR
HEATER	_____	THERE
VERBAL	_____	BRAVE
MEADOW	_____	MOWED
COURSE	_____	SCORE
NORMAL	_____	MOLAR
CARING	_____	GRAIN
HONEST	_____	STONE
RAMBLE	_____	REALM
HOARSE	_____	SHARE
EXTRAS	_____	TEARS

42 SNAKE CHARMER

Put the words below in alphabetical order and write them in the grid. Then read DOWN the starred column to answer this riddle:

What is a snake's favorite flavor of ice cream?

★

RESCUE

LESSON

BATHED

ZEROES

PLEASE

DESIGN

GRASSY

VISITS

SUNHAT

NECTAR

MIDWAY FUN

A midway is an area at a fair that has lots of fun booths and games. Find a path that visits all six attractions ONCE without visiting the same booth twice.

44 GOING IN CIRCLES

The Ferris wheel, invented by George Washington Ferris, first appeared at the Columbian Exposition in 1893. To find another name for this exposition, write down EVERY OTHER letter as you go clockwise around the Ferris wheel (you'll have to go around twice). The letters will spell out the answer.

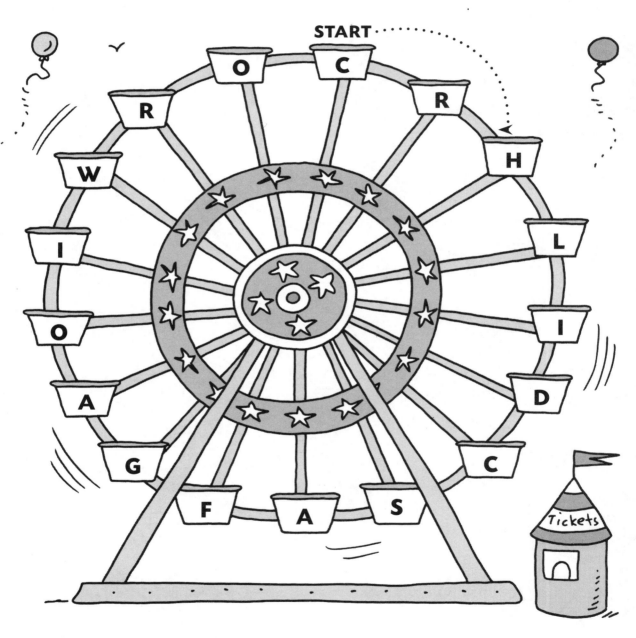

It was also known as the __ __ __ __ __ __ __ __,

__ __ __ __ __ __ __ __ __ __ __

66

SWEET TREAT

Put one letter into the blank space on each line to name a dessert you might eat at a county fair. Then read down the starred column to find another food that's really yummy.

ICE ___REAM

C___OKIE

CUS___ARD

DOUGHNU___

This treat is made out of sugar that's spun very fast.

BR___WNIE

MUFFI___

And it's very sticky.

CHO___OLATE CAKE

___PPLE CRISP

PUDDI___G

FU___GE

BLACKBERR___ PIE

SEE THE SIGHTS

See all the county fair sights using two dice
and a pencil! You can play alone or with a friend.

1. Roll the dice to try and match the number above each sight. You can use both numbers you roll OR the total of the two. For example, with a roll of 4 and 5, you can mark off sights #4 and #5 OR just sight #9.
2. Put your initials in ONE of the boxes under the sight you've chosen. If you can't use any of the numbers, your turn is over.
3. The winner is the first one to "visit" all nine sights.

Why are there so many little boxes under each picture?

So several players can play together, and so you can play more than once.

END OF THE LINE

Add one letter to the end of each group of letters to make a word that finishes each sentence. Then read DOWN to find a popular event at county fairs.

A baby sheep is a .... **L A M __**

Fairs often start with a .... **P A R A D __**

A domestic animal related to the camel is the ..... **L L A M __**

The first-place winner gets a blue .... **R I B B O __**

One organization for farm kids is the 4-H .... **C L U __**

The most popular ice cream flavor is .... **V A N I L L __**

Some fairs take place in a wooded .... **S E T T I N __**

The crafts show might be held in a canvas .... **T E N __**

Toddlers enjoy touching the animals at the petting ... **Z O __**

Some fairs end with a display of .... **F I R E W O R K __**

Tasty jams are made from .... **B L U E B E R R I E __**

INTO THE WOODS

Clever Challenges to Test You

DIFFICULTY RATING:
4 LOGS

FLOWER GARDEN

Sixteen flowers are hidden in the grid. Look across, up, down, diagonally (on a slant), both forward and backward for each one. Circle each flower when you find it. Reading from left to right and top to bottom, put the LEFTOVER letters into the blanks to find the answer to this riddle:

Why is the letter "A" like a flower?

ASTER
CARNATION
DAFFODIL
DAHLIA
IRIS
LILAC
LILY
NARCISSUS
ORCHID
PANSY
PEONY
PETUNIA
ROSE
SNAPDRAGON
SWEET PEA
TULIP

S	N	A	P	D	R	A	G	O	N
U	W	P	A	N	S	Y	I	R	O
S	T	E	S	T	N	F	D	C	I
S	I	O	E	O	L	L	A	H	T
I	O	R	E	T	W	E	H	I	A
C	T	P	I	D	P	B	L	D	N
R	U	Y	R	O	S	E	I	A	R
A	L	I	D	O	F	F	A	D	A
N	I	Y	L	I	L	I	L	A	C
B	P	E	T	U	N	I	A	E	E

Riddle answer:

___ ___ ' ___ ___ ___ ___ ___ ___

___ ___ ___ ___ ___ ___

TRAIL TRACKING

Can you find a path through the woods that visits all five spots exactly ONCE without traveling on the same path twice?

SYMBOL TALK

In this puzzle, letters and numbers stand for words. For example, T could stand for "tea," because that's how the letter sounds. They can be added together, too! M-T would be "empty" and B-10 would be "beaten." Can you figure out what's being said in each word balloon and then draw a line to the correct picture?

JOKING AROUND

Write the answer to each clue in the numbered blanks. Then move every letter to the same-numbered space in the box. Work back and forth between the clues and the box to find the answer to this riddle:

Why do squirrels hide in trees?

Camp "home" made of canvas ___ ___ ___ ___
19 16 22 1

Opposite of up ___ ___ ___ ___
31 2 7 30

Animal's hairy coat ___ ___ ___
10 18 27

Opposite of cold ___ ___ ___
24 28 14

What you see with ___ ___ ___ ___
25 9 4 20

Participate in a race ___ ___ ___
11 29 17

Small rug by a door ___ ___ ___
13 8 23

Farm animal with horns ___ ___ ___ ___
26 21 6 5

Pig ___ ___ ___
15 12 3

___ ___   ___ ___ ___   ___ ___ ___ ___
1 2   3 4 5   6 7 8 9

___ ___ ___ ___   ___ ___ ___
10 11 12 13   14 15 16

___ ___ ___ ___   ___ ___   ___ ___ ___
17 18 19 20   21 22   23 24 25

___ ___ ___ ___ ___ ___ ___ .
26 27 28 29 30 31

PICTURE THIS

SEE THE GREAT OUTDOORS WITH A CAMERA YOU CAN MAKE!

WHAT YOU'LL NEED:

A shoebox, pencil, scissors, tape, tracing or waxed paper, and a blanket.

This is called a pinhole camera. That's because instead of using a lens, all you have to do is poke a pinhole in your shoebox to see your pictures. Just follow the easy step-by-step instructions on these two pages.

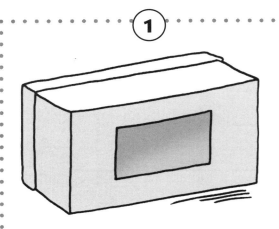

1 Get an adult to cut out a 4" x 5" rectangle on the bottom of your box.

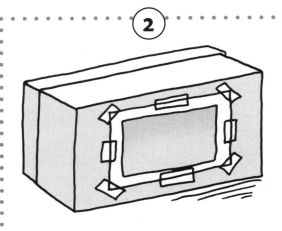

2 Tape a 6" x 7" piece of tracing or waxed paper over the window.

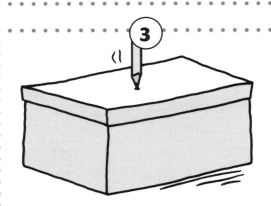

3 Turn your box right side up and poke a TINY hole in the top with a sharp pencil. (It should be about 1/16" wide.)

4 Tape the top on and decorate the box if you'd like. YOU NOW HAVE A CAMERA!

5

Go outside when it's sunny. Hold the box up with the back window of the camera facing you.

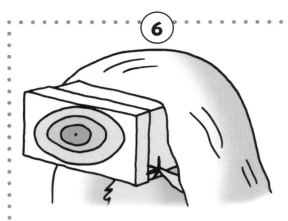

6

Drape a blanket over your head and the top of the box — but don't cover the pinhole!

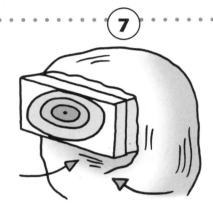

7

Wrap the blanket around the sides and bottom of the box to keep out as much light as possible.

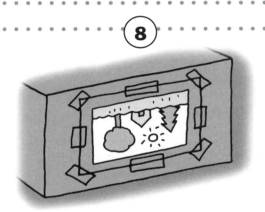

8

Take a look at the window. You'll see a picture of your surroundings! Brightly lit objects are easier to see.

HOW IT WORKS

Light waves travel from what you're looking at, go through the pinhole, and appear UPSIDE DOWN in your camera's back window.

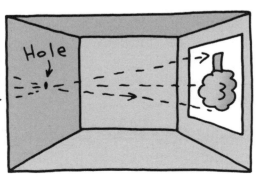

Here's what's happening inside your camera!

SYNONYM DISTRACTION

Fill in the blanks with a word that means ALMOST THE SAME as the word on the left. The new word answers the clue on the right.

	ANSWER	CLUE
AUTO	S _ _ _ LET CUP	Type of fungus
TAXI	SKUNK _ _ _ BAGE	Smelly plant found in wet areas
GUY	PRAYING _ _ _ TIS	Insect
EXTRA	SYCA_ _ _ _ _	Type of tree
RIPPED	_ _ _ _ A D O	Violent windstorm
BELOW	TH_ _ _ _ _ _	The sound that follows lightning
HELLO	_ _ BISCUS	Plant with large flowers

Aha! So a synonym is a word that means almost the same thing as another word.

Yes, like DUCK and SMART.

PARK SIGNS

Only two of these signs are exactly alike.
Can you find the matching pair?

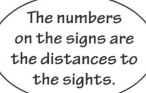

The numbers on the signs are the distances to the sights.

Ooh.

1
GEYSER...............5
WATERFALL.........11
SCENIC TRAIL.......4

2
WATERFALL...........5
GEYSER................10
SCENIC TRAIL......5

6
WATERFALL............5
GEYSER................11
SCENIC TRAIL.......5

3
GEYSER...............4
WATERFALL.........10
SCENIC TRAIL.......5

7
SCENIC TRAIL.......4
GEYSER...............10
WATERFALL...........5

4
WATERFALL............5
GEYSER................11
SCENIC TRAIL......5

8
WATERFALL............5
GEYSER................11
SCENIC TRAIL.......4

5
WATERFALL............5
GEYSER................11
SCENIC TRAIL.......4

9
SCENIC TRAIL.......5
GEYSER................10
WATERFALL...........5

MAPLE SUGAR LEAVES

Maple sugar leaves fall to the ground in the autumn. You can recognize them by their U-shaped notches and their smooth edges. All the words below are spelled using the letters in **MAPLE SUGAR LEAVES**.

Can you put each word into the grid on the next page? Start with the letters that are already in place and you will fill up the grid quickly.

3 Letters

EEL
SAP

4 Letters

GLUE
GULL
LESS
PEAR

5 Letters

AGREE
EASEL
LLAMA
PEARL
SMELL
SUPER

6 Letters

ASLEEP
LEAGUE
LEVELS
PLEASE

7 Letters

EARPLUG

GASP! PLEASE
SAVE ME!

How do you
do it, Buckley? Each
of those words uses
letters from MAPLE
SUGAR LEAVES!

OPPOSITE DISTRACTION

Fill in the blanks with a word that means the OPPOSITE of the word on the left. The new word you make answers the clue on the right.

	ANSWER	CLUE
OFF	HER _ _	Wading bird
AGAINST	_ _ _ EST	Area with lots of trees
HIGH	G _ _ _ WORM	Insect that gives off light
WOMAN	SALA _ _ _ DER	Amphibian similar to a lizard
STAY	_ _ PHER	Rodent with cheek pouches
PEACE	_ _ _ BLER	A bird that sings
HEALTHY	W _ _ _ OW	Tree with narrow leaves

REMEMBER!

Carefully study this scene for one minute, then turn the page and see how many of the questions you can answer.

REMEMBER! QUIZ

Now that you've studied the picture on page 83, answer these questions.

1. How many rocks are in the river?

   _____

2. Are Buckley and Daffodil hopping across the river on rocks or going across on a stone bridge?

   _____

3. What is Buckley carrying on his head?

   _____

4. How many trees can you see in the picture?

   _____

5. Is the sun in front of or behind Buckley and Daffodil?

   _____

6. How many frogs are in the picture?

   _____

No looking back!

7. What animal is sitting in one of the trees?

   _____

8. Is the fish that's jumping out of the water happy or sad?

   _____

LOVE LETTERS

Each creature mailed out one of these Valentine's Day cards. Can you figure out who mailed out which by reading the sayings and thinking "punny"? Write the number of the card above the creature that sent it.

A __

B __

C __

D __

E __

1 I'm HISS-TERICAL without YOU!

2 I LOVE YOU WITH MY HEART and SOLE

3 HAPPY VALENTINE'S DAY FROM YOUR CHILLED WREN

4 DEER MOM, I LOVE YOU

5 I'M NUTS ABOUT YOU

MISSING IN ACTION

Each of these popular birds is missing a three-letter word from its name. Take a word from the box and put it into the blank spaces to name the correct bird. Each word is used only once.

AND   CAN   CAR

HUM   KEY   PEN   ROB

ROT   ROW   TIN

S P A R __ __ __

__ __ __ D I N A L

N I G H __ __ __ G A L E

__ __ __ G U I N

P E L I __ __ __

P A R __ __ __

S __ __ __ P I P E R

__ __ __ I N

T U R __ __ __

__ __ __ M I N G B I R D

Now use the boxed words below to name ten insects.

CAT   DID   FIR

HOP   LAD   LOW   RAG

RAY   TIP   WEE

G R A S S __ __ __ P E R

Y E L __ __ __ J A C K E T

P __ __ __ I N G   M A N T I S

B O L L   __ __ __ V I L

__ __ __ E F L Y

__ __ __ Y B U G

C E N __ __ __ E D E

K A T Y __ __ __

__ __ __ E R P I L L A R

D __ __ __ O N F L Y

I'm a computer bug!

How come all my uncles are ants?

What kind of bug am I?

INSECT INFO

BUG ME!

INSECTS

BUGS 'R' US

87

SOMETHING'S FISHY!

Add the missing letter to make a word that finishes each sentence. Then read DOWN to find the name of a wildflower with pointed blossoms. It gets its unusual name from its leaves, which look like the color pattern of a certain fish.

When you walk in the woods you should follow a ___ **RAIL**

Snakes and lizards are ___ **EPTILES**

A bird with good vision and hearing is the ___ **WL**

Many animals live below the surface or ___ **NDERGROUND**

The noise caused by lightning is called ___ **HUNDER**

Sour green fruits are ___ **IMES**

A mosquito is an ___ **NSECT**

No, Daffodil, they mean a flower, not you!

A lake is a large body of water surrounded by ___ **AND**

Hey, I'm not yellow!

Daffodils are ___ **ELLOW**

TRAILSIDE TEASERS

Help Buckley and Daffodil solve these four brain teasers.

If the wind is blowing east, which way would a pine tree's leaves blow? Watch out! It's a trick question.

Can you draw this tent using only one line and without going over the same line twice? If you're having trouble, starting from a different spot — or use the hint below.

(Hint: Start at a bottom corner.)

Can you change the pyramid of pebbles on the left into the one on the right by moving only THREE pebbles?

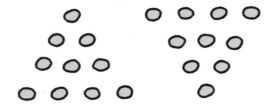

Try it using coins if you'd like.

Read this sentence aloud THREE times fast:

A BIRD IN THE THE BUSH

MIDDLE OF THE ROAD

Fill in the missing letter on each line to make a word that fits the clue. Then read DOWN the starred column to answer this riddle:

How do stinging insects talk to each other on the computer?

Clue	Word
Important liquid	W A __ E R
Is in pain	A C __ E S
Use a broom	S W __ E P
Head of a city	M A __ O R
Sixty-minute periods	H O __ R S
Stinging insects	W A __ P S
Not dirty	C L __ A N
Log house	C A __ I N
Costing very little	C H __ A P
Perspire	S W __ A T
Animal with a hump	C A __ E L
Absence of war	P E __ C E
Playground equipment	S L __ D E
Young male horses	C O __ T S

90

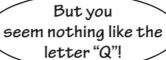

Hey, lookie, I'm a trail guide!

But you seem nothing like the letter "Q"!

Now do the same thing to find the answer to this riddle:

Why is the letter "Q" like a trail guide?

⭐

Grin	S M __ L E
Timepiece worn on a wrist	W A __ C H
Striped wild animal	T I __ E R
Got up	S T __ O D
Visitor	G U __ S T
Sloppy	M E __ S Y
Piece of furniture	T A __ L E
Use an iron	P R __ S S
Saltwater candy	T A __ F Y
Gets bigger	G R __ W S
Birthday event	P A __ T Y
Small brown birds	W R __ N S
Small rodent	M O __ S E

LET'S HAVE A PICNIC

Seventeen picnic items are hidden in the grid. Look across, up, down, and diagonally (on a slant), both forward and backward for each item. Circle each one when you find it. Reading from left to right and top to bottom, put the LEFTOVER letters into the blanks to find the answer to this riddle:

On what day do kids drink the most water at picnics?

CAMERA
CHAIRS
CUPS
DESSERTS
DRINKS
FRUIT
GAMES
NAPKINS
PLATES
RADIO
SALADS
SANDWICHES
SUNSCREEN
TABLE
TOYS
UMBRELLA
UTENSILS

```
S  O  D  E  S  S  E  R  T  S
E  U  M  B  R  E  L  L  A  A
T  T  N  N  T  A  B  L  E  N
A  E  A  S  R  I  A  H  C  D
L  N  P  T  C  D  U  H  A  W
P  S  K  I  S  R  R  R  S  I
T  I  I  G  A  M  E  S  F  C
O  L  N  T  D  M  A  E  Y  H
Y  S  S  R  A  D  I  O  N  E
S  P  U  C  D  R  I  N  K  S
```

Riddle answer:

_____ _____ _____ _____

UP A MOUNTAIN

Tough Teasers to Show
How Smart You Are

DIFFICULTY RATING:
5 LOGS!

ANNA'S GRAM

Anna's Gram (Grandma) likes to write silly phrases for Anna. She takes a word like MOUNTAINS and moves the letters around to make UNITS MOAN. Each phrase on the right uses ALL of the letters from one of the words on the left. Write the number of each phrase on the blank next to the word it came from.

A. ALLIGATOR _____

B. BUTTERFLY _____

C. CHICKADEE _____

D. EARTHWORM _____

E. HIBERNATE _____

F. MIGRATION _____

G. MILLIPEDE _____

H. MISTLETOE _____

I. PORCUPINE _____

J. SAGEBRUSH _____

1. PILED LIME

2. RIP POUNCE

3. MATH ROWER

4. LARIAT LOG

5. TRY ELF TUB

6. SOME TITLE

7. BREATHE IN

8. HUGE BRASS

9. OMIT GRAIN

10. IDEA CHECK

IT'S A TWISTER!

Each of these tongue-twisters is missing one word. Find the correct word from the list below and write it in the blank. Then try saying the tongue-twister three times fast.

BROKEN CREEK FILLED GRASS OTTER THREE WILL

GREEN _____ GROWS FAST

BUCKLEY BROUGHT HIS _____ BUCKET

DAFFODIL'S _____ BILL

GREAT GREEK _____

THROW THESE _____ THROUGH TREES

_____ WILD WEEDS WILT?

WATER GOT THE HOTTER _____ WETTER

These tongue-twisters have gotten my tongue all tied in knots.

Mmmthh oothhhh!

CLOSE RELATIVES

Change the underlined letter in each word to find three related words or phrases in each group. Write your new words on the lines. Buckley and Daffodil did the first one for you.

BODIES OF WATER

BAKE   _____LAKE_____

FOND   _____

TEA   _____

PARTS OF A FLOWER

METAL   _____

STE**P**   _____

LEA**P**   _____

FISH

TU**B**A   _____

PUPPY   _____

HER**D**ING   _____

CAMPING EQUIPMENT

BENT   _____

S**W**EEPING B**I**G   _____ _____

LATER B**A**TTLE   _____ _____

TREES

<u>A</u>LIVE _____

WEE<u>D</u>ING <u>P</u>ILLOW _____   _____

A<u>M</u>PLE _____

INSECTS

<u>P</u>LEA _____

<u>S</u>LY _____

M<u>A</u>TH _____

FISHING GEAR

<u>M</u>OLE _____

<u>C</u>ACKLE <u>P</u>OX _____   _____

<u>W</u>AIT _____

RODENTS

<u>W</u>EAVER _____

<u>R</u>UT _____

<u>H</u>OUSE _____

TANGLED TREE

This has got to be the world's twistiest tree!
Can you find the way from START to END?

ONE, TWO, THREE

Follow the three steps below to find the answer to this riddle:

What do insects drink in the woods?

1. Read each clue and add the letters needed to spell the answer. (Two letters are in place to guide you.)
2. Write the letters that have numbers below them on the same-numbered dashes below.
3. Read across for the answer.

I'm thirsty!

CLUE   ANSWER

Not early: __ A T __
              4

Baby dog: __ U P __ __
           2   3

"Beauty and the _____":   B E __ __ __
                   1

Finished: __ O N __
          9   5

Opposite of rich: __ __ O R
            7

Cab: __ A X __
              8

The color of clouds: __ __ I T __
                 10

Female sibling: __ I S __ __ __
       6   11

__ __ __ __ __   __ __ __ __ __ __
1   2   3   4   5   6   7   8   9   10   11

HIKE TO THE TOP

Find and circle SEVEN things on the next page that are different from the mirror image on this page. Extra credit: Can you find an EIGHTH? It's pretty tricky (well, we think so anyway)!

FUN WITH PUNS

THISTLE (this will) be a fun puzzle if you think in a "punny" kind of way. Choose a word from the box that sort of makes sense in one of the spaces below. It helps to read the sentences aloud.

CANOE	**HONEYBEE**	**LEAF**
LETTUCE	**ORANGE**	**PETAL**
TULIPS	**WEEVIL**	**WORM**

1. STOP BOTHERING ME. JUST _____ ME ALONE.

2. _____ COME ON A HIKE WITH US?

3. YOU HAVE _____ JUST BELOW YOUR NOSE.

4. TURN ON THE FAN. IT'S _____ IN HERE.

5. I HOPE _____ MEET AGAIN.

6. _____ IN! WE'RE FREEZING OUT HERE.

7. _____ NICE AND HOLD THE DOOR OPEN.

8. MY _____ BE GOOD. HE WON'T BARK.

9. _____ YOU GLAD YOU CAME TO THE BARBECUE?

JUST JOKING

The answers to these jokes have been written using pictures, letters, and words. Some of them have to be added together to make words.

How do porcupines play leapfrog?

How do you keep a snake from striking?

RULES, RULES

Oops! A raccoon tore out 16 words from the official WOODS WALK rule sheet. Put each word into its correct spot so the rules make sense. Cross off each word after you use it.

AN   AT   BAG   HE

LACE   LEASE   LIFE   LIT

LOW   RAIL   RASH   SAFE

SHE   SON   THE   YOU

P_____   FOL_____   ____SE
RULES FOR ____R _____TY

• DO NOT DISTURB T___
  WILD_____.

• DO NOT ____TER. P_____
  T_____ IN GAR____E CANS.

• STAY ON THE T_____.

• W___CH OUT FOR SNAKES,
  WILD ___IMALS, AND
  POI____ IVY.

• KEEP PETS ON LEA____S.

PUNCH LINE-UP

Write the letter of the correct punch line in the space next to each joke.

1. ___ What was the rabbit's favorite type of dancing?

2. ___ What animals grow down as they grow up?

3. ___ What's the largest ant in the world?

4. ___ A man rode to the fair on Friday. Two days later, he left on Friday. How is this possible?

5. ___ What do porcupines say when they hug?

6. ___ What birds are always sad?

7. ___ Why don't seagulls live near bays?

8. ___ What did the lake use to say goodbye to the trees?

9. ___ If you have 5 apples in one hand and 4 in the other, what do you have?

A. Waves

B. Big hands

C. Blue jays

D. Because then they'd be called bagels

E. Geese

F. Ouch!

G. Antarctica

H. Hip-hop

I. Friday was his horse

HO HO HEE HEE HA HA!

DOUBLE TROUBLE

The names of 11 SEA CREATURES and 10 FRUITS are mixed together in this list. Each word will fit into one spot in one of the grids on the next page. You have to figure out which one. Start with the letters that have been filled in already and put each word into its correct spot. Cross off each word after you write it in the grid.

3 Letters

COD
EEL
FIG

4 Letters

PEAR
TUNA

5 Letters

APPLE
BERRY
GRAPE
PEACH
TROUT
WHALE

6 Letters

BANANA
MARLIN
MINNOW

7 Letters

ABALONE
APRICOT
HADDOCK
HALIBUT

8 Letters

MACKEREL

9 Letters

NECTARINE

10 Letters

CANTALOUPE

107

SIXERS

Put TWO three-letter word fragments from the box together to make a six-letter word that answers each clue. Write the answer in the grid going DOWN. Read the letters in the gray squares from 1 to 8 to answer this two-word riddle:

How much is a skunk worth?

ACO	BOB	CAT	EAM
GAR	GES	ING	LOD
MON	OLE	ORI	RNS
SAL	SPR	STR	TER

CLUES

1. Brightly colored bird
2. The season before summer
3. Places where beavers live
4. Fish that swim upstream

5. Wild animal
6. Type of snake
7. Nuts from oak trees
8. Small body of water

1	2	3	4	5	6	7	8

SOUND OFF

Read each word and think of a homophone for it. Write the homophone in the grid. Then read down the starred column to find the answer to this riddle:

What is a tree's least favorite month?

A homophone is a word that sounds the same as another word but is spelled differently and has a different meaning.

CREAK and CREEK are homophones.

1. HOARSE

2. DEAR

3. PAUSE

4. TENSE

5. TALE

6. MISSED

7. BARE

8. HAIR

9. ORE

SILLY SKUNK QUIZ

Circle the correct answer to each of these multiple choice questions.

1. The scent gland liquid from some skunks is used to make:
A. orange juice   B. cafeteria food   C. perfume   D. pancake syrup

2. Which of these isn't a type of skunk:
A. hognose   B. spotted   C. striped   D. pink polka-dotted

3. Skunks can make good pets if:
A. they live in another state   B. their scent glands are removed
C. you have no sense of smell   D. you like smelling really bad

4. About the farthest skunks can spray their scent is:
A. one inch   B. 15 feet   C. two football fields   D. to the moon

5. Which of these is NOT a danger to skunks:
A. coyotes   B. great horned owl   C. ants   D. automobiles

6. Skunks are nocturnal, meaning they're most active during:
A. fire drills   B. the Super Bowl   C. the night   D. school recess

7. Spotted skunks can spray directly over their heads by:
A. doing a handstand   B. using a spray can of "Skunk Juice"
C. magic   D. using mirrors

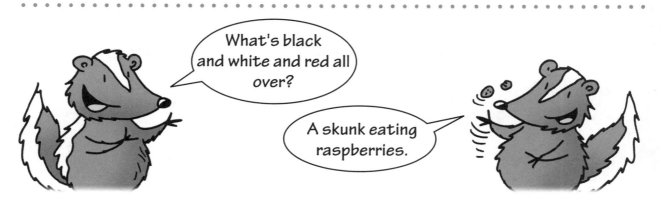

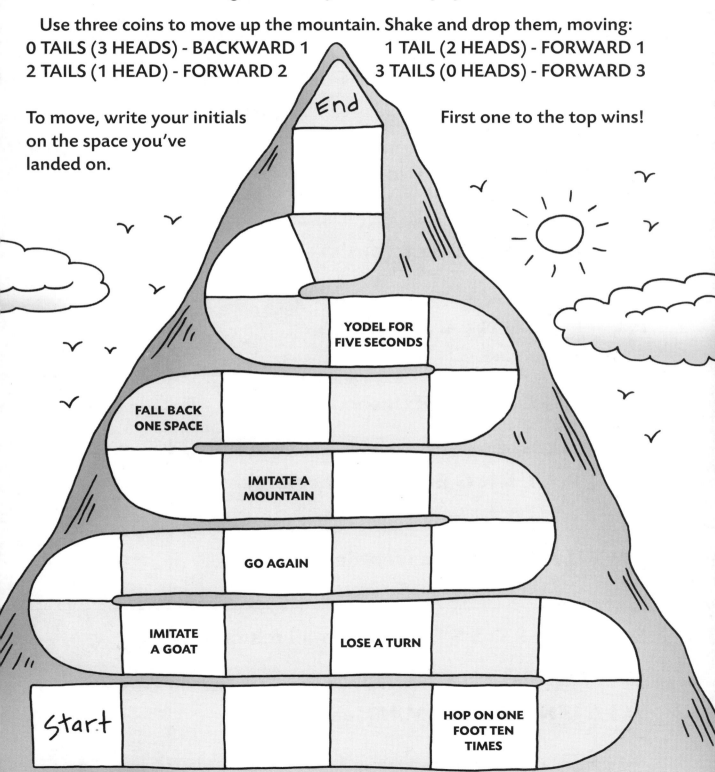

MOUNTAIN CLIMBER

A fun game for any number of players.

Use three coins to move up the mountain. Shake and drop them, moving:

0 TAILS (3 HEADS) - BACKWARD 1   1 TAIL (2 HEADS) - FORWARD 1

2 TAILS (1 HEAD) - FORWARD 2   3 TAILS (0 HEADS) - FORWARD 3

To move, write your initials on the space you've landed on.

First one to the top wins!

End

YODEL FOR FIVE SECONDS

FALL BACK ONE SPACE

IMITATE A MOUNTAIN

GO AGAIN

IMITATE A GOAT

LOSE A TURN

Start

HOP ON ONE FOOT TEN TIMES

WORD WEAVING

Two related words are woven together on each line. The letters of each word are in the correct order; your job is to separate them. The words in ( ) give you a clue to what you're looking for. Example:

G R M U A S D S (Nest materials)

GRASS _____   **MUD** _____

V D I A O L I S E T Y (flowers)

_____   _____

S P D A R O V R O W E (birds)

_____   _____

H E P I M L O N E C K (trees)

_____   _____

C R M O I C T K E T H (insects)

_____   _____

Y E O R A L L N G E O W (leaf colors)

_____   _____

S N T U A R T K E L E (reptiles)

_____   _____

O P W E A S O S S E L U M (small mammals)

_____   _____

W I A U N T E T U R M N (seasons)

_____   _____

THE GREAT OUTDOORS DICTIONARY

A dictionary and word quiz in one!

On the next four pages are some words that appear in this book. Most are words from the great outdoors, but a few aren't.

Cover up the definitions (on the right) and see how many words you know without looking. Close enough counts!

Put a check mark in the box next to every word you get right, then see how you rate on page 118.

- [x] **Acorn** — Nut from an oak tree.
- [ ] **Albatross** — Large seabird.
- [x] **Alligator** — Large reptile with thick, tough skin.
- [x] **Bean bag toss** — Game using bags filled with beans that are thrown through holes in a board.
- [x] **Butterfly** — Insect with large, brightly colored wings.
- [x] **Centipede** — Crawly creature with many legs.
- [ ] **Chickadee** — Small bird named for the sound of its call.
- [x] **Chipmunk** — Small brown animal with a striped back.
- [x] **Compass** — An instrument that shows directions.
- [x] **Cotton candy** — Pink, spun sugar twirled onto a stick.
- [x] **County fair** — Yearly event featuring crafts, farm foods, games, rides, and livestock shows.
- [x] **Earthworm** — Worm that lives in the soil.
- [ ] **Exposition** — Big show or fair.
- [x] **Fern** — Flowerless plant that often grows in dark and wet places.
- [x] **Forest** — Large area filled with trees and plants.
- [x] **Fungus** — Growth such as mold, mildew, or a mushroom.

- [x] **Funnel cake** — Doughy treat with powdered sugar on it.
- [x] **Glowworm** — Insect that gives off light (a firefly).
- [x] **Gopher** — Small mammal that tunnels underground.
- [x] **Grasshopper** — Insect with powerful legs that it uses for jumping.
- [x] **Hare** — Animal like a rabbit but with longer ears.
- [ ] **Heron** — Long-necked, long-legged wading bird.
- [x] **Hibernate** — To sleep for a long time (bears hibernate in the winter).
- [ ] **Hibiscus** — Bush with large, brightly colored flowers.
- [x] **Honeybee** — Bee that makes honey.
- [x] **Livestock show** — Event where farm animals are judged.
- [x] **Lodge** — Den for beavers.
- [ ] **Midway** — Area at a fair with booths and games.
- [x] **Migration** — Animals moving from one place to another at certain times of the year.
- [x] **Millipede** — Crawly creature with many legs.
- [x] **Mockingbird** — Bird that imitates other birds' songs.
- [x] **Morse code** — Message system that uses dots and dashes instead of letters.

☑	**Moss**	Growth found on rocks and tree trunks.
☑	**Nocturnal**	Most active during the night.
☐	**Oriole**	Brightly colored songbird.
☐	**Pika**	Small mammal with short ears.
☑	**Poison ivy**	Plant whose oil can cause an itchy rash.
☑	**Porcupine**	Animal with long, sharp quills.
☑	**Praying mantis**	Long, green insect (while resting it looks as if it's praying).
☐	**Purple martin**	Large bird with purple-blue feathers.
☑	**Reptile**	Cold-blooded animal with scaly skin.
☑	**Road runner**	Large, fast-moving bird with a long tail.
☑	**Rodent**	Animal with large, sharp front teeth used for gnawing.
☑	**Sagebrush**	Bushy shrub that grows in dry areas.
☑	**Salamander**	Amphibian that looks like a lizard.
☐	**Scarlet cup**	Type of fungus.
☐	**Sequoia**	Very tall evergreen tree.
☑	**Silhouette**	Black outline drawing.
☑	**Skunk cabbage**	Smelly plant found in wet areas.

☐	**Stork**	Wading bird with a long bill.
☑	**Sudoku**	Type of grid puzzle.
☑	**Sunscreen**	Lotion that protects against sunburn.
☑	**Swallow**	Small, swift bird with a forked tail.
☑	**Sycamore**	Tree with smooth bark.
☐	**Tackle box**	Box that holds small fishing gear.
☑	**Thistle**	Prickly, flowering plant.
☑	**Tornado**	Strong wind storm.
☐	**Trout lily**	Wildflower with speckled leaves.
☐	**Vireo**	Small, grayish or greenish songbird.
☐	**Warbler**	Small songbird.
☐	**Weevil**	Small beetle that damages crops.
☑	**Willow**	Tree with narrow, drooping leaves.
☑	**Yellowstone**	Largest and oldest national park in the United States
☐	**Yew**	Smallish evergreen tree or shrub.

How many words did you know?
Count up all the check marks, then turn the page . . .

THE GREAT OUTDOORS DICTIONARY

HOW DID YOU DO?

There are 64 words in the dictionary. Count one point for every one you knew and see how you rate:

10	GOOD
20	GREAT
30	FABULOUS
40	ABSOLUTELY AM-A-A-A-ZING!
50	HELLO, BRAINIAC
60	WE'RE BEYOND STUNNED

If you got them all, your name must be John James Audubon! (He was a famous bird painter, but he also painted animals and filled his backgrounds with many of the trees and plants he saw in his travels.)

THE ANSWERS

① A COUNTRY STROLL

1 ROCKY ROAD
Page 10

2 TAKE A HIKE
Page 11

```
            F
    M       L                   C
B A C K P A C K               O
    P       S                   M
            H                   P
            L         F         A
            I         O         S
H I K I N G B O O T S
            H         D
        W A T E R
```

3 CHECK THIS OUT
Page 12

ANSWER:

WHAT MOVIE DOES A REPTILE LIKE BEST?
THE LIZARD OF OZ

4 DON'T TOUCH
Page 13

ANSWER:
POISON IVY

1. Pumpkin   P
2. Owl   O
3. Igloo   I
4. Sock   S
5. Orange   O
6. Nest   N

7. Iron   I
8. Violin   V
9. Yarn   Y

5 ODD ONE OUT
Page 14

ANSWER:

TRUNK

6 NEST MATERIALS
Page 15

7 IN THE POND
Page 16

ANSWER:
You wouldn't normally find a TUB, KITE, PENCIL, HOSE, or (especially) FIRE in a pond.

8 POND VISITOR
Page 17

9 ORDER! ORDER!
Page 18

10 THREESIES
Page 19

ANSWER:
A "BUTTER" FLY

11 LOOK AROUND
Pages 20-21

12 WHAT IS IT?
Page 24

15 BIRDS IN THE SKY
Page 27

13 EYE CATCHERS
Page 25

ANSWER:
VIREO

14 FINE DINING
Page 26

ANSWER:
FRENCH FLIES

16 MOVE IT
Page 28

ANSWER:
CHOCOLATE CHIRP (CHIP)
COOKIES

② ACROSS THE CREEK

17 RAFTING FUN
Page 30

18 BIRD-WATCHING
Page 31

ANSWER:
BINOCULARS

		A	L	B	A	T	R	O	S	S			
B	L	U	E	B	I	R	D						
		C	A	N	A	R	Y						
		D	O	V	E								
		M	O	C	K	I	N	G	B	I	R	D	
R	O	A	D	R	U	N	N	E	R				
		S	W	A	L	L	O	W					
				J	A	Y							
	P	U	R	P	L	E	M	A	R	T	I	N	
				S	T	O	R	K					

19 ROAD HOG
Page 33

ANSWER:
A PIG UP (PICKUP) TRUCK

TAXICAB	A
POLICE CAR	P
FIRE ENGINE	I
DUNE BUGGY	G
BUS	U
JEEP	P
TRACTOR	T
TRICYCLE	R
AMBULANCE	U
CAR	C
DIRT BIKE	K

20 UNDERWATER
Pages 34-35

21 JUST BEE-CAUSE
Page 36

ANSWERS:

1.
What is a bee's
favorite country?
Stingapore (Singapore)

2.
What do you call a
bee that does not brag?
A humble bee (bumblebee)

22 MESSAGE CENTER
Page 37

ANSWER:
BY MOSS
(MORSE)
CODE

A	B	O	U	T
B	U	Y	E	R
C	L	I	M	B
D	O	Z	E	N
E	R	A	S	E
F	I	R	S	T
G	E	C	K	O
H	O	R	S	E
I	D	E	A	L
J	U	I	C	E

23 "R" YOU READY?
Page 38

ANSWER:

Rainbow, rain, raft, rock, rope, raccoon, rabbit, and rooster.

We didn't intend raincloud to be an answer, but you can count that if you got it. Also, even though Buckley and Daffodil are poling, we'll accept rowing.

24 TREE TOPS
Page 39

ANSWER:

THEY RACED AROUND THE TRACK.	CEDAR
IS THE HERO A KIND PERSON?	OAK
CAN YOU SPIN EIGHT TOPS?	PINE
HIS PEN PAL MIGHT VISIT.	PALM
LUCY PRESSED A HANDKERCHIEF.	CYPRESS
WHO HAS PENCILS FOR THE TEACHER?	ASPEN
WHICH RECIPE CAN YOU MAKE?	PECAN
WHERE IS THE TEA KETTLE?	TEAK
I'LL BE THERE IF I REMEMBER.	FIR
WHERE WILL I MEET YOU?	LIME

25 CREATE A COMIC
Pages 40-41